SALISBURY
IN OLD PHOTOGRAPHS

SALISBURY
IN OLD PHOTOGRAPHS

COLLECTED BY
PETER SAUNDERS

ALAN SUTTON
1987

Alan Sutton Publishing Limited
Brunswick Road · Gloucester

First published 1987

British Library Cataloguing in Publication Data

Salisbury in old photographs.
1. Salisbury (Wiltshire)—History
I. Saunders, P.R.
942.3'19   DA690.S16

ISBN 0-86299-413-6

Typesetting and origination by
Alan Sutton Publishing Limited.
Printed in Great Britain
by Redwood Burn Limited.

CONTENTS

INTRODUCTION

Photography has enabled individual moments in time to be captured for posterity since the 1840s, and many hundreds of photographs of Salisbury have survived down through the decades since then. The collection in this book is a representative sample of some of those photographs. They range from the remarkably early views of the Market Place, including a view of the Dinner commemorating the Crimean Peace in 1856, to within a generation of the present. Any selection will inevitably reflect the interests of the compiler as well as the availability and technical suitability of the prints themselves, but I hope that the scenes of city life, personalities and events depicted here will stimulate and entertain others as they have me.

The arrangement of the photographs is based on subject matter rather than chronology, but the subject sections are themselves fairly arbitrary: it is possible here to find a trademan's delivery van under 'Transport' or 'Trade'; a wedding group under 'People', 'Events' or 'The Close'. Each of the photographs will also convey a different meaning to different individuals depending on their age, interests, memories and familiarity with Salisbury. Taken together as a collection they provide a unique visual history of Salisbury's more recent past.

Salisbury, or New Sarum, has been a market centre and cathedral city since the thirteenth century. Its chequers (formed by a grid pattern of streets) with the Market Place as a focus, and the Cathedral Close, have given Salisbury a character of its own which has fortunately survived in large measure the developments of recent years which have so altered the face of many a town. Nevertheless these photographs are a record of change. The Market House in the Cheesemarket, for example, whose façade alone now survives on the Salisbury Library is remembered by many Salisbury folk, but it can only be a photograph, not living memory, which brings before us the building demolished to make way for it in 1958.

Changes in society, fashions, customs and attitudes, are also revealed by these photographs, especially in the sections on 'Events', 'People' and 'Leisure'. The appeal of subscription events and public rejoicing, especially in Victorian and Edwardian days, is clearly seen in the photographs depicting jubilee dinners and processions in the 'Events' section where organised gatherings and the decoration of the City take place on a scale seldom seen in Salisbury today.

Although 'The Close' has a section to itself, the Cathedral is such a photogenic symbol of Salisbury that I have endeavoured to avoid giving it undue prominence here, for, to the majority of Salisbury's citizens, 'Streets' and 'Trade' will have had a greater relevance in their everyday lives.

In the 1920s the City Council appointed an Ancient Buildings Committee. It commissioned and collected photographs of buildings. These became known as the Lovibond Collection, and of its 306 prints 25 appear in this book. My gratitude for the use of these, and the sources of the many other photographs appear in 'Acknowledgements'. Here, however, we should pause before looking at their work to remember all those photographers who produced the originals from which those in this book were copied. The work of such photographers as H.C. Messer of Castle Street, Witcomb and Son of Catherine Street, and F.G.O. Stuart of Southampton is especially important, but photographers who are now anonymous also deserve our admiration, some for the quality of their work, all for their contribution to Salisbury's visual history. Most of the photographers would no doubt be surprised that the otherwise transient images which they captured on film would become valuable historical records.

Streets and Buildings

THE HIGH STREET in 1945. Note the Fifty Shilling Tailors and the continuing use of horse-drawn vehicles. The Shoulder of Mutton Inn was demolished in 1962.

HIGH STREET decorated for Queen Victoria's Diamond Jubilee in 1897, W.H. Smith & Sons have now replaced the Assembly Rooms.

HIGH STREET in the 1880s.

THE MAYOR AND CORPORATION IN PROCESSION to a thanksgiving service at the cathedral on VE Day, 1945.

HIGH STREET LOOKING NORTH TO ST THOMAS CHURCH decorated for Queen Victoria's Diamond Jubilee in 1897.

MARKET PLACE, 1850s or 1860s. Photography had not reached Salisbury in 1838!

THE MARKET PLACE, C. 1900.

MINSTER STREET AND THE CHEESEMARKET with the London City and Midland Bank acting as a recruiting office during the First World War.

OX ROW AND MARKET PLACE, in the late 1940s.

BLUE BOAR ROW DECORATED IN 1897 FOR QUEEN VICTORIA'S JUBILEE. The imposing façade of the Wilts and Dorset Bank is little changed today as Lloyds Bank.

THE CHEESEMARKET showing the Maidenhead Inn, replaced in 1858 by the Market House.

THE POULTRY CROSS, *c.* 1890.

THE POULTRY CROSS in the 1930s. The only shop still trading there now is Olivers shoe shop.

BINGHAMS DRAPERY STORE in 1893. Now Wimpey's.

NEW STREET, August 1924.

SHEEP BEING DRIVEN DOWN THE CANAL from Milford goods station past carriers buses lined up in 1921.

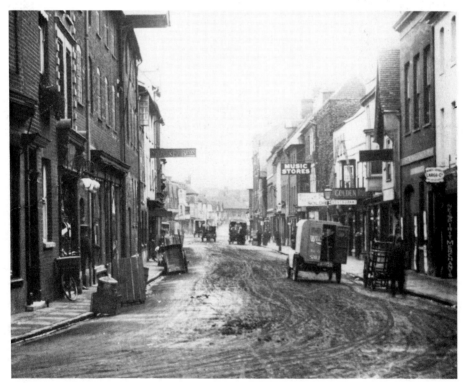

NEW CANAL, c. 1918.

THE CANAL. The photographer's carriage adds interest to the scene.

THE CANAL, decorated in 1897 for Queen Victoria's Jubilee.

ST JOHN'S STREET. There's that carriage again!

CATHERINE STREET IN THE EARLY 1920s.

CRIPP'S TEA & GROCERY WAREHOUSE and the Red Lion Hotel, c. 1935.

WESSEX MOTORS SHOWROOMS at the junction of New Street and Catherine Street in the late 1920s.

L.J. SLY, GOLDSMITH & JEWELLER, 52 BLUE BOAR ROW, established in 1850 and still thriving into the twentieth century.

'SLY'S CORNER' after 1935.

CHIPPER LANE in 1928. The Castle Auction Mart is now a Tesco Supermarket.

WINCHESTER STREET. Little has changed since the First World War except the names. Kite's is now Wong's Chinese takeaway!

ST ANN STREET, C. 1907.

ST ANN STREET, C. 1895. The New Inn is now the Tollgate Inn.

CORNER OF THE CANAL AND QUEEN STREET, C. 1928.

THE 'ROUND OF BEEF', Milford Street, in the 1920s.

47 WINCHESTER STREET and St Edmund's Church Street, in the 1920s.

THE NEW INN AND YE OLDE HOUSE, restored by the antique dealer, Charles Scamell, in the 1920s.

SILVER STREET in the 1920s. Chaplin's horse-drawn carrier makes the scene look earlier. The aroma of tobacco from N. Stevens & Co's shop is now but a memory.

BELLE VUE, 76 ENDLESS STREET with the Salisbury Volunteer Fire Brigade in 1902.

THE PALACE THEATRE on the junction of Endless Street and Chipper Lane in the 1920s.

LONDON ROAD, c. 1905. Now Escourt Road.

THE JUNCTION OF WILTON ROAD WITH DEVIZES ROAD, pre-First World War.

THE LONDON AND SOUTH WESTERN RAILWAY BRIDGE, 1906.

SUMMERLOCK BRIDGE, Fisherton Street before its alteration and rebuilding in 1901.

RADNOR HOUSE, YORK ROAD. Now demolished, it was part of Fisherton County Gaol until 1870, and from 1901 it was used as the Headquarters, Second Army Corps, later Southern Command.

FISHERTON STREET IN THE FLOODS OF 1915.

THE SITE FOR THE POST OFFICE built in 1905 on the corner of Castle Street and Chipper Lane.

THE RISING SUN INN, CASTLE STREET, 1908.

EARLY TWENTIETH CENTURY CHILDREN enjoying a rest on the Greencroft, bought and laid out for public recreation in 1883.

CIVIC DIGNATORIES at the opening of the Council House in St Edmund's College, bought by the City in 1927.

THE SEVENTEENTH CENTURY STAIRWAY in the yard of the Plume of Feathers Inn, later the Turkish Baths, now incorporated in the Cross Keys pedestrian mall, late nineteenth century.

THE BLACKMORE MUSEUM, opened 1867.

THE INFIRMARY before 1892 when Dr John Roberts built the clock tower upon the remains of the former County Gaol.

SNOW CLEARING, 18 January 1881, 'probably in Castle Road'.

EXETER STREET, c. 1930.

OLD SARUM VIEWED FROM THE BISHOPDOWN TRACK, the old Castle Inn is just visible, c. 1900.

MEYRICK AND CECIL AVENUES, off Coombe Road, in 1905.

HARNHAM ROAD in the days when children played with hoops in the street.

PANORAMIC VIEW OF SALISBURY FROM HARNHAM HILL, 1897. The chalk pit and a cricket match appear in the foreground. From a glass negative 'doctored' with wheat ears.

HARNHAM OR AYLESWADE BRIDGE in the early twentieth century. From the 1240s until 1931 when New Bridge was built, all traffic going south passed over this bridge.

COTTAGES IN EAST HARNHAM, with inquisitive children, 1897.

AERIAL VIEW OF THE CITY, c. 1930. The Market Place, St Thomas' Church and the Poultry Cross stand out. The Bus Station and the Old George Mall are still developments of the future.

FROM THE CATHEDRAL SPIRE LOOKING NORTH WESTWARD ACROSS THE CLOSE, Long Bridge, the nurseries where Queen Elizabeth Gardens now are, steam engines beyond Churchfields and the Nestle's chimney in smoke.

QUEEN STREET. By Edwardian days the lime trees to commemorate Queen Victoria's 1887 Jubilee were growing well.

SILVER STREET , busy in the 1930s.

The Close

ST ANN'S GATE, C. 1900, with W. Witt's blacksmith's forge and A. Harwood's bakery delivery cart visible through the arch.

ST ANN'S GATE at the turn of the century.

HARNHAM GATE, C. 1900.

HIGH STREET CLOSE GATE in the late 1880s.

LOOKING OUT THROUGH THE HIGH STREET CLOSE GATE, c. 1900.

THE CATHEDRAL in the 1890s.

JANE FISHER AT THE AGE OF THREE with her doll, 'Minnie' outside Mompesson House in 1909.

NORTH WALK APPROACHING CHORISTERS GREEN, by Ladywell. The pillar box survives, but the setting of trees, creepers, and domestic servant in cap and apron have gone.

THE CLOSE DID NOT ESCAPE THE FLOODS OF 1915.

A VICTORIAN FAMILY AT 17 THE CLOSE.

A SALISBURY CHORISTER.

CATHEDRAL CHORISTERS boating on the Avon in the 1920s.

CATHEDRAL STONEMASONS in the 1860s.

MR T. RATTUE AND TWO STEEPLEJACKS in 1921 with the weather vane of 1762, which it was his job to oil.

GEORGE BOYLE, DEAN OF SALISBURY, 1880 –1901, with his domestic staff.

DR PAGE ROBERTS, Dean of Salisbury
1907–1919, in the Deanery garden.

VIEW ALONG THE NORTH WALK, c. 1910.

MR W. SEWILL, a pawnbroker, on his Minerva motorcycle taking his daughter round the close.

THE TOWNSEND FAMILY LANDAU with coachman/gardener A.E. Barons, c. 1900, outside Mompesson House.

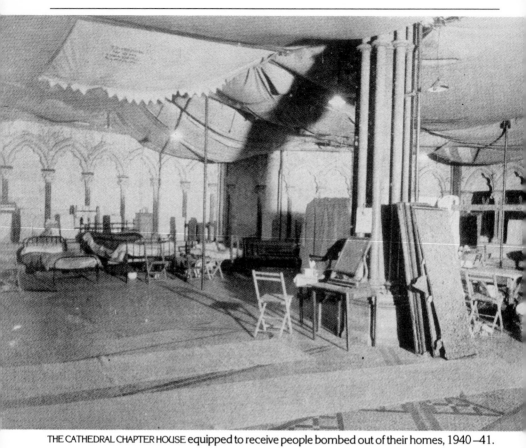

THE CATHEDRAL CHAPTER HOUSE equipped to receive people bombed out of their homes, 1940–41.

People

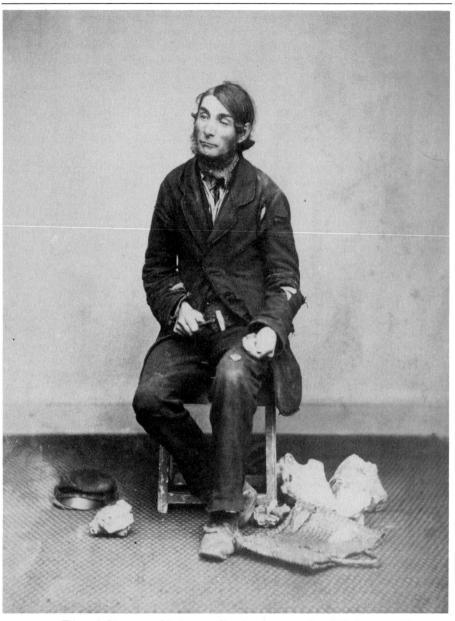

'FLINT JACK', Edward Simpson, fabricating flint implements for E.T. Stevens, Honorary Curator of the Salisbury and South Wiltshire Museum, in 1863.

THE SALISBURY GIANT outside the Museum in St Ann Street in 1887 with Hob Nob.

THE BEVERAGE COMMITTEE, on the steps of the Council House, was responsible for the provision of 800 gallons of beer drunk at the Market Place public dinner held in 1902 to celebrate the Coronation of Edward VII.

THE MAYOR AND CORPORATION IN FISHERTON STREET, 1902.

W.H. BAILEY, AS A BOY, C. 1870. He owned a bookbinder's shop in Queen Street, later run by his son, Harry.

REVIEW OF JUNIOR SEA SCOUTS IN THE GUILDHALL SQUARE in 1902. The statue of Sidney Herbert commemorates the MP for South Wiltshire who was Secretary of State for War duing the Crimean War. It was removed to Victoria Park to make way for the 1914–18 war memorial.

GINA HAMMICK AND TED FISHER at Mompesson House after their marriage on 9 May 1905.

THE ASSIZE COURT JUDGE led in procession from The Close by the 'javelin man', c. 1922.

FIRST BATTALION, WILTSHIRE REGIMENT in the County March, 1913 approaching the Market House.

A WEDDING AT ST THOMAS'S CHURCH, c. 1918. The groom and guard of honour are all war wounded.

THE YMCA SATURDAY FOOTBALL TEAM, c. 1910. T.E. Adlam, front left, won a VC in 1916.

SALISBURY CITY POLICE in 1905. The moustache was clearly in vogue.

67

JO OSMOND, who ran the cab rank outside the Infirmary before the First World War, seen here at the railway station.

MR GEORGE PENNY, horse dealer, in Ox Row, c. 1920.

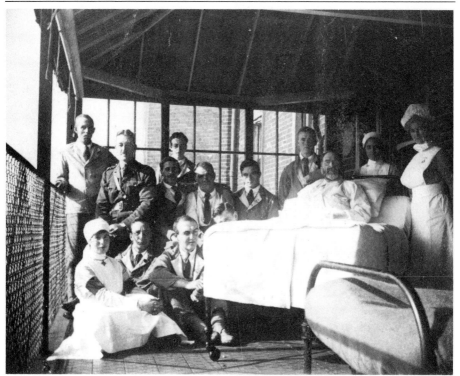

CAPT. C. NOTELY AND WAR WOUNDED recovering in the Infirmary, 1917.

A CHILDREN'S WARD IN SALISBURY INFIRMARY
in 1945.

MISS PHYLLIS JORDAN AND MISS M. SMITH AS AIR RAID WARDENS during the Second World War. Miss Jordan was in charge of the gardens and Miss Smith a Lecturer in infants education at the diocesan Training College, King's House.

SALISBURY'S AUXILIARY FIRE SERVICEMEN in September 1941.

THE WILTSHIRE REGIMENT (DUKE OF EDINBURGH'S) received the freedom of the City, 3 December 1947.

FIELD MARSHALL VISCOUNT MONTGOMERY OF ALAMEIN arriving in the Market Place on 14 December 1949 to receive the Honorary Freedom of the City.

A SALISBURY WORKING-CLASS FAMILY at tea in the mid 1940s.

FULFORD PLACE, off Castle Street,
typical of poorer homes in the 1920s.

A SALISBURY MIDDLE-CLASS HOME in the mid 1940s.

A FAMILY PICNIC at the time of Queen Victoria's Golden Jubilee, possibly on Harnham Hill, June 1887.

SECTION FOUR

Trade

THE MARKET, pre-1856. One of the earliest photographs of the Market Place known and taken through a studio lens. From a damaged glass negative.

THE MARKET PLACE, c. 1900.

THE MARKET IN THE 1850s when cattle were permitted untethered.

THE MARKET PLACE in the late 1930s.

MAIN & SONS, MINSTER STREET. Now Kentucky Fried Chicken.

FISHERTON MILL in the nineteenth century.

WILTSHIRE CHEESE MERCHANT, MR ARNOLD (in white coat) who sold cheese in the 1850s and 60s on the site of the medieval Cheese Cross, near the present Library.

THE MARKET HOUSE with its impressive iron and glass roof built in 1858.

THE HALL OF JOHN HALLE, the Canal, c.1910 when Watson's China Shop. In 1931 it became the Gaumont Palace Cinema.

WILKES & SON, IRONMONGERS, on the corner of Milford Street and Queen Street, c. 1890.

H.R. TRIBBECK, WATCHMAKER AND JEWELLER, 61 Silver Street, decorated for George V's Coronation, 1911. Herbert Tribbeck is third from the right.

THE YORK ROAD BRANCH OF THE CO-OPERATIVE SOCIETY, c. 1919.

GREENS FISHMONGERS, 47 Fisherton Street. Concealed for many years, the remains of the façade are now visible again.

MR WILLIAM PERCY'S WYNDHAM DAIRY IN HAMILTON ROAD.

G. REDMAN, FAMILY BUTCHER, Winchester Street in 1922.

STEVENS, DRAPER, MILLINER & OUTFITTER, 55–59 Silver Street before 1927 when it became Woolworths.

H.J. ANNETTS, China Stores, 35 Silver Street, in 1930.

ROBERT STOKES SCOUT DELIVERY VAN outside the Canal entrance to his shop. On the back of this van was stated 'Teas blended, coffees roasted to suit the waters of the neighbourhood'.

THE HOUSE OF JOHN A 'PORT, WATSONS, Queen Street, decorated for Queen Elizabeth II's Coronation, 1953.

THE CANAL in the 1920s. Peter Lord's shoe shop makes Clark & Lonnen and Geo. Hill & Son unrecognisable today.

MACFISHERIES, HEPWORTHS AND MAYPOLE SHOPS IN SILVER STREET in the early 1930s. These household names still seem familiar today though they are gone from Salisbury.

BOOTS THE CHEMIST SHOP IN THE CANAL in the 1920s.

W.J. SNOOK & CO., FAMILY BUTCHERS, at the junction of High Street and Silver Street in the 1920s.

THE SWAN INN BY AYLESWADE BRIDGE, EAST HARNHAM, c. 1897. Mrs Ridout's donkeys which pulled her carrier, the 'Coombe Express', traditionally stopped at this inn to share her pint of ale.

3 & 5 FISH ROW in the late 1920s. The family butcher, A. Pritchett, still provides 'high class English meat' now as then, though Bedford, the florist and fruiterer, closed soon after.

RICHARDSON BROTHERS, WINE AND SPIRIT MERCHANTS. In 1897 its cellars housed '60,000 bottles of wine ready for immediate delivery.' It is now Barclays Bank and the County Hotel.

PAIN, LEWER & CO'S BREWERY, Castle Street, c. 1875. Now Tesco's.

SUMMERLOCK BRIDGE AND THE WAGON AND HORSES INN, Fisherton Street, pre-1858.

THE PHEASANT INN, SALT LANE, c. 1910.

JOHN FOLLIOTT & SONS, BREWERS, Rollestone Street, c. 1900.

GIBBS MEW & CO, c. 1930, has stood the test of time!

T. BLACKBOURN'S BELL FOUNDERS, the Friary, with a bellframe made for Petherton Church in Somerset in 1896.

FELTHAMS SHOEING FORGE, St Ann Street in the late 1920s.

MR HARRY TILL, SADDLER AND LEATHER CRAFTSMAN, at work in his Brown Street premises in May 1945.

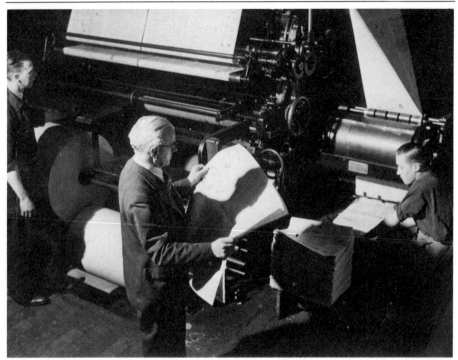

THE *SALISBURY TIMES* coming off the presses in 1945.

THE ELECTRICITY GENERATING STATION housed in the Town Mill, 1945.

SECTION FIVE

Events

THE CELEBRATION IN THE MARKET PLACE OF THE PEACE after the Crimean War, 20 May 1856. This remarkably early photograph enables others taken in the Market Place to be dated. Note that it predates the Market House and shows the building next to The Chough being demolished. Market Dinners were to continue to the Coronation of George V in 1911.

THE SALISBURY GIANT, HOB NOB AND MORRIS DANCERS as they appeared for Queen Victoria's Golden Jubilee, June 1887.

THE FIRST WILTSHIRE RIFLE VOLUNTEERS about to fire the *feu de joie* in the Guildhall Square before the Procession celebrating Queen Victoria's Jubilee, June 1887.

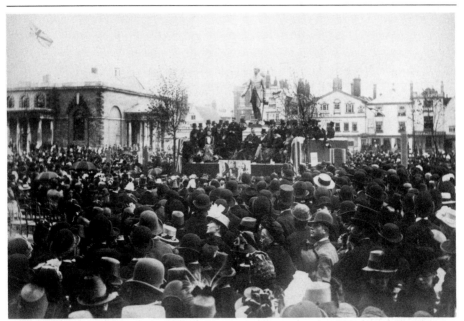

UNVEILING THE STATUE OF HENRY FAWCETT IN THE MARKET PLACE in 1887. Henry Fawcett, the blind Postmaster-General, was born in Queen Street.

FISHERTON STREET WITH TRIUMPHAL ARCH proclaiming the advent of free wiring. The Salisbury Electric Light and Supply Co. opened in the Town Mill in 1899.

BLUE BOAR ROW IN 1897 during the procession for Queen Victoria's Diamond Jubilee.

THE MEN'S DINNER IN THE MARKET PLACE, Queen Victoria's Diamond Jubilee, 1897. Vibert's shop was burnt down in 1901.

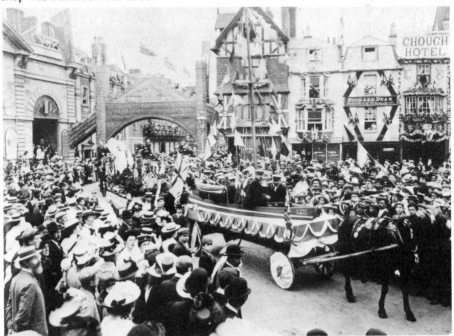

THE PROCESSION FOR KING EDWARD VII'S CORONATION, 1902, entering Blue Boar Row.

THE MEN'S DINNER IN THE MARKET PLACE, Edward VII's Coronation, 1902.

BRIDGE STREET with the procession for Edward VII's Coronation, 1902. Every vantage point is taken up.

THE GIANT, HOB NOB AND MORRIS DANCERS, with Mayor J. Folliott, on the occasion of the celebration of the Coronation of Edward VII, 1902.

KING EDWARD VII AND QUEEN ALEXANDRA arriving at the station, 27 June 1908.

EDWARD VII AND QUEEN ALEXANDRA entering the Wilton Road *en route* for Wilton House.

FISHERTON CONSERVATIVE CLUB'S FLOAT 'BRITANNIA' preparing for King George V's Coronation procession, 1911.

THE GIANT falling over in Fisherton Street during the procession for the Coronation of George V, 1911.

THE GIANT IN EXETER STREET for the Children's Peace Festival Pageant Procession, 28 July 1919.

THE GIANT in Kelsey Road preparing for the procession to mark Queen Elizabeth II's Coronation, 1953.

THE STEAM BOAT EXPRESS TRAIN FROM PLYMOUTH derailed at the L & SW station on 1 July 1906. Twenty eight lives were lost.

PROCESSION IN BLUE BOAR ROW, June 20 1906, *en route* to the first Hospital Fête at Victoria Park.

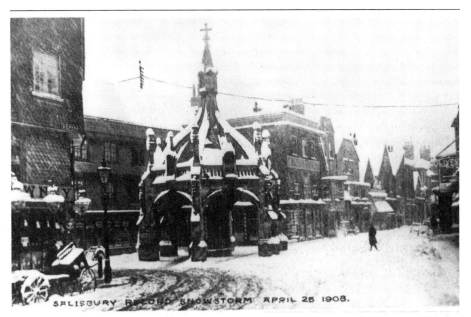

THE POULTRY CROSS AND BUTCHER ROW in Salisbury's 'record snowstorm', 25 April 1908.

CEDAR TREE AT MILFORD HALL, Castle Street, damaged by snow in the storm of 1908. The house on the right is now the site of Caffyns Garage.

THE GUILDHALL SQUARE ON EMPIRE DAY, 1909.

FISHERTON STREET, flooded 5 January 1915. A helpful police constable lends a hand delivering bread.

MILL ROAD DURING THE FLOODS OF 1915.

TANK IN CATHERINE STREET IN WAR BOND WEEK, 5 March 1918.

TANK IN THE GUILDHALL SQUARE, 5 March 1918, for War Bond Week. It could almost be a scene from an Eastern bloc country. The Sebastopol cannon went for the war effort in 1942.

THE VOLUNTEER FIRE BRIGADE demonstrating their steam fire engine 'Alert' in Blue Boar Row. 1 May 1907.

THE VOLUNTEER FIRE BRIGADE demonstrating their hose power based on the 'Alert' steam fire engine, 1 May 1907.

B. VIBERT AND CO, Grocers, Wine & Spirit Merchants. The shop was destroyed by fire in 1901, allowing a rare glimpse directly through from Oatmeal Row to Minster Street.

THE CLOCK FACTORY FIRE, 27 May 1909.

SALISBURY STEAM LAUNDRY, SALT LANE, destroyed 12 June 1922.

FIREMEN FIGHTING THE SALISBURY CO-OPERATIVE SHOP FIRE on the corner of Milford Street and Queen Street on 13 September 1937. The shop was gutted but the Cathedral Hotel saved.

IMPROMPTU DANCING in the Guildhall Square on VE Day, 1945.

THE MAYOR, A.E. BATT, AND COUNCILLOR A.A. MAIDMENT, looking heavenward, inspecting a Civil Defence and Food Flying Squad demonstration in the Guildhall Square, 18 October 1957. © Crown Copyright 1987.

SECTION SIX

Transport

FISHERTON TURNPIKE TOLL-GATE HOUSE, demolished c. 1860, and St Paul's Church.

THE LONDON AND SOUTH WESTERN RAILWAY FIRE ENGINE outside the Great Western railway station, manned by railway employees for Queen Victoria's Golden Jubilee Procession, June 1887.

THE TOLL GATE IN NELSON ROAD, where to pass on foot cost ½d.

SCAMELL'S BRIDGE UNDER CONSTRUCTION in 1898. The bridge and Nelson Road were to connect the Wyndham Road area with Fisherton and the railway stations.

JOHN LAMPARD CARRIAGES IN EXETER STREET.

THE WHITE HART HOTEL'S CARRIERS CART in about 1914 used for delivering London and South Western railway parcels.

DIOCESAN TRAINING COLLEGE FOR SCHOOLMISTRESSES, King's House, The Close, c. 1905.

THE AIRSHIP 'BETA' which had 'been flying over the city several times' on military manoeuvres in 1910.

EDWARDS GARAGE IN HIGH STREET in c. 1905.

FREDERICK PAPPS driving the hearse he leased to E.J. Harrison, undertaker in High Street, c. 1915. It was made by Scout Motors with bodywork by Farr, both of Salisbury.

HOPKINS & SON HORSE WAGONS at their Imperial Aerated Water Works in Castle Street, c. 1914.

GIBBS, MEW & CO. LTD'S FIRST MOTOR CARRIAGE, a 1912 Thornycroft two-tonner, loaded here at its Anchor Brewery, Gigant Street.

H.J. SUTTON'S WATERLOO FLOUR MILLS FODEN STEAM LORRY, C. 1906, loaded apparently for a staff outing.

JOHN LAMPARD DRIVERS with their ex War Dept lorries at their Harnham Depot in 1924.

MR SAM SMITH ON HIS HENDERSON MOTOR CYCLE of 1913, advertising his Music Stores at 78 Fisherton Street.

SALISBURY'S FIRST MOTOR FIRE TENDER outside the fire station in Exeter Street, 1913.

A FARLEY AND DISTRICT MOTOR SERVICES DENNIS BUS with bodywork by Farr of Salisbury, registered in April 1914.

WILTS & DORSET MOTOR SERVICES SCOUT known for obvious reasons as the 'greenhouse', on the Amesbury–Woodford–Salisbury route in the Market Place, c. 1916.

CANN'S WILTON ROAD SERVICE STATION, c. 1929.

THE BUS STATION, ENDLESS STREET, in 1945.

THE LONDON TRAIN at Salisbury station in 1945.

VOLUNTEERS FOR THE M.R.C. COMMON COLD UNIT AT HARVARD HOSPITAL being collected from Salisbury station, c. 1946.

Leisure

VICTORIA PARK laid out in 1887, as the Jubilee Recreation Ground to mark Queen Victoria's Golden Jubilee.

BROKEN BRIDGES BETWEEN HARNHAM AND BEMERTON, c. 1906.

RIVERSIDE WALK by the Avon behind Castle Street.

AUDIENCE AT A 'TEBBY'S CONCERT PARTY' IN VICTORIA PARK, C. 1910. Mr Tebby is standing wearing a straw hat.

CROQUET PARTY IN THE GARDEN OF MOMPESSON HOUSE in the 1860s. 'Jinny' Townsend lived in Mompesson House and wrote in her diary for 18 July 1863: 'We played croquet in the afternoon and were all photographed in a group. The Hall party came & Mr Buckle & Mr Gregory & Grace. I think it will come out very good.'

THE PAVILION, VICTORIA PARK, crowded with spectators during the sports celebrating Edward VII's Coronation in 1902.

A TUG OF WAR, one of many activities in Victoria Park during the celebrations of Edward VII's Coronation in 1902.

THE WOMEN'S TEA PARTY IN VICTORIA PARK held to celebrate the Coronation of Edward VII saw the consumption of a ton of cake and 50 lbs of tea.

THE MEN'S DINNER IN THE MARKET PLACE, Edward VII's Coronation, 1902. Ladies and children had to watch from windows and rooftops.

SALISBURY VOLUNTEER FIRE BRIGADE FOOTBALL TEAM which beat Salisbury Police, three goals to two, 10 April 1912.

SALISBURY LADIES SWIMMING CLUB at the pool behind the Town Mill in 1917.

SUNDAY SCHOOL, CHURCH, CLUB AND WORKS OUTINGS were very popular in the 1920s and 1930s. This one, c. 1927, is setting off from The Canal.

A CHARABANC OUTING TO BOSCOMBE, Bournemouth, organised by the Salvation Army, ready to set off from Blue Boar Row, 13 June 1923.

THE OCTOBER FAIR, c. 1890.

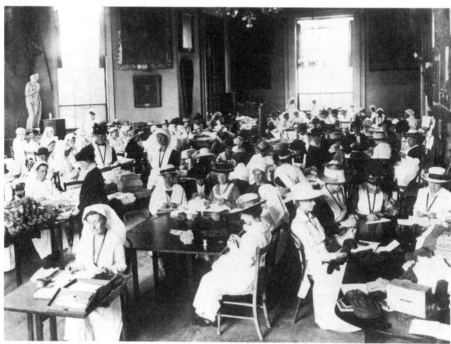

QUEEN MARY'S NEEDLEWORK GUILD SEWING PARTY in the Guildhall during the First World War.

THE OCTOBER FAIR, c. 1930.

Salisbury
Electric Palace

THE PALACE THEATRE, Endless Street, opened as the County Hall in 1889, showed films from 1910 and closed in 1931.

THE STAFF OF THE PICTURE HOUSE, Fisherton Street on Peace Day 21 July 1919 when a stalls seat could be had for 9*d* (less than 4p). In 1943 it became the Garrison Theatre, and in 1953 the Playhouse.

ENTRANCE FOYER AND PAYBOX OF THE NEW PICTURE HOUSE, 22 August 1947.

FRANK PAYNE AND HIS 'COSMOPOLITANS' BAND.

'THE MODERNIQUES' DANCE BAND in 1948.

A REHEARSAL OF A GUILDHALL CONCERT PARTY, 1945.

SALVATION ARMY CITY BAND IN HIGH STREET in 1953, a reminder that the Salvation Army band was founded in Salisbury.

Learning and Worship

ST EDMUND'S COLLEGIATE SCHOOL, BOURNE HILL, in 1876, founded by the Revd G.H. Bourne who acquired the College mansion in 1873. In 1875 he bought the playing field opposite Wyndham Terrace, and until his death in 1925 cared for the grounds attached. Bourne Hill was subsequently named after him.

THE GODOLPHIN SCHOOL, MILFORD HILL, c. 1900.

WYNDHAM ROAD AND ST MARK'S SCHOOL, c. 1910.

FISHERTON INFANTS SCHOOL, CLASS 3, in 1914.

CHORISTERS AT LESSONS in the cathedral school (Wren Hall) in the 1940s.

CHORISTERS AT PRACTICE WITH SIR WALTER ALCOCK, cathedral organist, in the 1940s.

DIOCESAN TRAINING COLLEGE FOR SCHOOLMISTRESSES, King's House, The Close, c. 1880. Now the Salisbury Museum.

MEALTIME AT THE TRAINING COLLEGE, c. 1905.

THE ARCHBISHOP OF CANTERBURY with the Bishops of Salisbury, Bristol, Southwark and Bath and Wells laying the foundation stone of the Chapel of the Holy Angels at the Training College, 11 July 1898.

ST ANDREW'S CHURCH, BEMERTON at the turn of the century.

THE CHURCH OF ST THOMAS OF CANTERBURY, c. 1900.

THE CHOIR OF ST THOMAS'S CHURCH posed outside the church tower's belfry door.

THE GUILD OF HOLY OBEDIENCE, SARUM ST MARTIN'S, before 1894.

THE MAUNDREL HALL, FISHERTON STREET. Opened in 1880 by public subscription as a meeting-place for undenominational worship and discussion, especially for the poor, and named after the Protestant martyr, John Maundrel. Now an Argos showroom.

THE PRIMITIVE METHODIST CHAPEL, FISHERTON STREET during the floods in January 1915.

MAYOR C.J. WOODROW laying the foundation stone of the Carnegie Public Library, 4 November 1904. Note the domestic staff straining to view this closely guarded civic occasion!

EXCAVATIONS IN 1864 OF A GRAVEL PIT at Milford Hill cricket pitch produced a 'good flint implement'.

General View of Excavations at Old Sarum.

THE INNER BAILEY OF OLD SARUM during the excavations of 1909–1915.

THE INTERIOR OF THE BLACKMORE MUSEUM with Mr E.T. Stevens, its Hon. Curator. The Museum housed a remarkable collection of material from the Americas and prehistoric objects from Europe.

MR FRANK STEVENS showing visitors a medieval key in the Salisbury, South Wiltshire and Blackmore Museum just after the Second World War.

ACKNOWLEDGEMENTS

The pleasure of compiling this book has been made the greater by the very willing assistance of all those who have lent photographs, provided technical help and offered advice or encouragement.

My thanks go especially to the Trustees of the Salisbury and South Wiltshire Museum, whose archive provided half of the photographs, and to Mr Dave Cousins and Mr Peter Daniels for their unstinting practical contributions.

Equally the following helped me in various ways or lent and gave permission to reproduce photographs:

D.J. Algar; R. Annetts; Miss E. Barnard; Frances Bassett, Southampton Reference Library; British Council; J. Cox; Suzanne Eward, Salisbury Cathedral Library; Mrs N. Jupe; Mrs F. Kenney; Janet Kenyon, National Museum of Photography; Ministry of Agriculture, Fisheries and Food; Major John Peters and Justine Taylor, Duke of Edinburgh's Royal Regimental Museum; Alan Richardson; Lynn Rivers; Salisbury District Council, especially Mrs J. Pearce and D. Rawlinson; Mrs E. Sanger; Eleanor Saunders; R. Seal; N. Skelton; R. Spring; Miss Carola Stuart, Michael and Hilary Wrench, National Trust; Mrs Penelope Sykes; R.H. Till; R. Tribbeck; Dr David Tyrrell and Mrs K. Callow, MRC Common Cold Unit; Mrs Jane Walford; Wiltshire County Council Library & Museum Service, Director and staff, especially John Chandler, Edward Boyle and Lynn Wootton; Wiltshire Record Office, especially Ken Rogers, John d'Arcy and Mrs M. Moles.